CW01433510

Original title:
The Spirit's Guiding Lantern

Author: Ophelia Ravenscroft
ISBN HARDBACK: 978-3-69081-094-4
ISBN PAPERBACK: 978-3-69081-590-1

Glow of Endless Horizons

In the dark, I lose my shoe,
Trip over shadows, then boo-hoo.
A flash of light, I gasp and squeal,
A raccoon dancing with zest and zeal.

A guiding glow on my dinner plate,
It's just the fridge light—oh, what fate!
I swear it winked, like it knows my plight,
Got leftovers? Let's party all night!

Courageous Illuminations

On a quest for snacks, I bravely roam,
In the pantry's depths, feel far from home.
But a flicker calls me to check it out,
Turns out it's just my cat, without a doubt!

The flick of a switch sets the mood just right,
Now I can see I'm still in my nightlight.
With every shimmer, a giggle I stow,
Tonight we feast, just me and my glow.

Gleam of Distant Dreams

In a land where lost socks gather,
There shines a bulb, oh what a blather!
It whispers secrets of all things bright,
Like how to bake cookies without a fight.

A twinkling wink from a distant star,
It says, 'You're close, but just not far!'
I follow the gleam, full of delight,
Right to my fridge, oh what a sight!

Shimmering Threads of Light

When in doubt, just spin around,
Like a disco ball—now that's profound!
Each shimmer a step, I dance with glee,
While my dog's rolling, laughing at me.

With glowing threads that weave and twine,
I've lost my way, but that's just fine.
A laugh, a grin, all in good cheer,
As I trip over a lamp, oh dear!

The Light That Never Fades

In a world where socks disappear,
A glow appears to chase the fear.
It speaks in jokes, it tells a pun,
Light-hearted laughter, oh what fun!

Each step a wiggle, each twist a turn,
Chasing shadows, we laugh and learn.
In kitchens bright or halls of cheer,
It's guiding all who wander near.

An unexpected dance brings joy,
Even when we stumble, oh boy!
With every chuckle, we're never lost,
This guiding glow, it counts the cost.

Souls Alight in Stillness

In quiet corners where we play,
A flicker brightens up the gray.
The coffee spills, the chaos reigns,
But humor lingers through the pains.

With every sigh, a punchline's born,
As wisdom sprinkles with the scorn.
Our mismatched socks become the stars,
In stillness laughter heals the scars.

So bring your quirks, your quirks and glee,
For silly moments set us free.
In gentle nudges, life takes flight,
A crazy dance in soft moonlight.

Glimmers of Truth in the Abyss

In the depths where worries stew,
A shimmer sparkles just for you.
It tickles thoughts, it clears the mist,
With every giggle, life's a twist.

What's hiding there beneath the gloom?
A joke awaits to fill the room.
The shadows rumble, laughter swells,
In this abyss, our humor yells.

A silly face, a fun parade,
In deep waters, we won't be swayed.
The truths revealed in jestful rhyme,
Make every moment worth the climb.

The Lantern at the Crossroads

At every turn, we pause and grin,
A lantern flickers, let's dive in.
With every chuckle, paths collide,
In mismatched shoes, we take the ride.

Which way to go? Oh, what a plight!
But who cares? We'll laugh all night!
With silly stunts and joy on repeat,
We'll find the way with dancing feet.

Decisions made with laughter loud,
A merry band, we're all so proud.
The crossroads sparkles, never fades,
As our sides ache from all the jades.

The Luminescent Guide

In the dark, I lost my way,
A shadow danced, come what may.
It wiggled, jiggled, made me laugh,
Like a beacon, with an awkward staff.

I followed it through fields of green,
A silly sight, oh what a scene!
Tripped on the root of a giant shoe,
The guide just chuckled, 'What's wrong with you?'

Rays of the Uncharted

Beneath the stars, the map was wrong,
But my flashlight sang a quirky song.
It blinked in Morse, a chatty glee,
'Go left, go right, just follow me!'

The rays shone bright, a glowing crew,
With silly hats and colors too.
They led me to a hidden store,
Where snacks and laughs meant wanting more.

The Fire of Inspiration

A flickering flame lit up my dreams,
It whispered jokes, or so it seems.
"Why did the chicken cross the light?
To find the punchline, what a sight!"

With giggles bright, I danced around,
While neighbors peeked, a joy unbound.
"Just a fire," I said, with a grin,
"Who knew brilliance could make me spin?"

Illuminated Tales

Stories flickered in colors bold,
With laughter mixed like tales of old.
A knight with a cat, oh what a show,
His armor sparkled, as if on glow.

The dragon snorted, a sneeze so grand,
It blew the knight across the land.
Not a fight, but a playful chase,
Together they giggled, a silly race!

Heavenly Wayfinder

In the sky, a map is drawn,
With arrows made of cheese and brawn.
Stars are winking, what a tease,
Navigating with such hilarious ease.

Comets zoom like crazy cars,
While planets sing like disco stars.
I steer my ship with jelly beans,
And laugh at all my silly dreams.

Glimmering Threads of Fate

A string entwines from here to there,
Tangled up in cosmic hair.
Pull one end, the other yawns,
Out pops a cat in polka-dots!

Rabbits hop with woozy grace,
Weaving laughs in outer space.
Each bounce a giggle, swift and bright,
In the tapestry of silly night.

The Flame of Discovery

A candle flickers, dims a bit,
Then does a little happy split.
It dances close, then far away,
Oh, light that loves to jest and play!

Marshmallows roast, they laugh too loud,
As popcorn bursts, it's quite a crowd.
Each pop a secret, sweet delight,
In the warmth of giddy light.

Light's Silent Song

A glow that hums a cheeky tune,
Beneath a smirk of cheeky moon.
It winks at clouds, does a twirl,
Leaving all the stars in a whirl!

It tickles shadows, makes them dance,
While giggling halls invite a prance.
Every beam a chuckle, bright,
Echoing through the joyful night.

Illuminated Journeys

In the night of wobbly dreams,
A light that giggles and beams.
It points the way to pizza pies,
And shows where all the socks disguise.

With flashes bright like fireflies,
It leads us to the best surprise.
Around the corner, funny hats,
And dancing cats with silly spats.

A guide so quirky, how bizarre,
It dances like it's gone too far.
We follow where the glow expands,
Through lands of rubber bands and pans.

In every laugh, there's wisdom true,
Even if the jokes seem askew.
So let us prance, embrace the twirl,
As lanterns laugh and colors swirl.

Ethereal Threads of Light

In whimsical threads that spin and spin,
A sparkling glow where jokes begin.
It ties the sly and cheeky gnome,
To find his way back to his home.

With every wink and funny grin,
It leads us where the laughs begin.
Through meadows filled with giggling bees,
And rivers flowing with silly sneeze.

It strings together all the fun,
As giggles rise like bubbles spun.
A guide with a feather in its hat,
Dancing with a clown and a chat.

With every blink, it winks at fate,
As laughter and joy collide in spate.
Follow the glow and cast aside,
Your fears are lost on this wild ride.

Radiance Beyond the Veil

Beyond the veil where shadows play,
A glow that tickles night and day.
It whispers jokes in the dark delights,
Igniting giggles and dazzling sights.

Through wobbly paths where pancakes fall,
It guides us to the grandest ball.
With lively tunes from goofy hearts,
As we partake in silly arts.

It twirls us round, a light ballet,
Where troubles bounce and dance away.
A beacon bright in quirky hues,
With charts that lead to funny news.

The glow delights in comic schemes,
We chase the light and follow dreams.
With every jig, we laugh aloud,
Lost in the glow, we feel so proud.

Illuminating Wisdom in Darkness

In shadows thick where silliness hides,
A twinkling light that always bides.
It tickles thoughts with every spark,
Turning the twists into a lark.

With insights wrapped in giggly glee,
It shows us how to just be free.
In every riddle, jokes unfold,
As wisdom glows like threads of gold.

Through every stumble, we can laugh,
With riddles that can change your path.
It guides our hearts to silly fun,
Chasing shadows until we run.

In every twist, a truth we seek,
With light so bright, it helps the weak.
So let us trip, let joy ignite,
In laughter's glow, we'll find our light.

Emissaries of the Luminescent Path

With a giggle, they flicker bright,
Casting shadows that jump in fright.
Chasing echoes, they dance and zoom,
Lighting up the midnight room.

Wobbling like they've had too much,
Stumbling with a playful touch.
Guiding folks through paths of glee,
Laughter ringing, wild and free.

Twilight's Embrace of Light

As stars twirl in a cosmic game,
They whisper secrets, never the same.
A winking glow from every leaf,
Brings giggles and joyous belief.

In the dusk, they weave and sway,
Making mischief in their own way.
A flash here, a glimmer there,
Jokes unleashed in the evening air.

Light Through the Mist

Through the fog, they tease and play,
Guiding wanderers, come what may.
A spark of mischief, quick and sly,
Making shadows laugh and sigh.

"Follow me!" they wink and spin,
Leading lost folks grinning in.
With every turn, they toss a jest,
Mirthful beacons, simply the best.

Beacon of the Unseen

A wink and glimmer in the night,
They prance with joy, a silly sight.
Invisible threads of laughter weave,
In every corner, they believe.

With every flicker, a giggle bursts,
In shadows deep, humor thirsts.
So follow on, with hearts so light,
Join the dance of pure delight!

The Inner Beacon

In a room full of socks,
One's gone on a stroll,
It winks like a star,
While I chase my own shoal.

The fridge hums a tune,
As I dance with delight,
Eggs roll with a laugh,
In my kitchen's twilight.

A mismatched pair grins,
Playing hide-and-seek,
Even the dust bunnies,
Join in the cheeky peek.

With giggles and quirks,
I'm led by a glow,
A beacon of joy,
Wherever I go.

Light of Ancients

The old lamp's awake,
Whiskers tickle the shade,
Bringing tales of yore,
In a riddle parade.

The candles join in,
Their dance is a spree,
While shadows play pranks,
On the walls, oh so free.

A laugh from the past,
Squeezes out of the light,
It whispers old jokes,
Till we giggle outright.

In the warm, glowing hue,
History's wacky show,
In each flickering beam,
Fun stories to bestow.

Kaleidoscope of Hope

Colors swirl and spin,
In a laughter brigade,
Each hue tells a tale,
As a joke is replayed.

The world's full of whim,
Through that prism, I see,
A rainbow of chuckles,
And some silly glee.

With giggles in pockets,
I bounce on my feet,
Life's a wacky ride,
With surprises to greet.

Hope twinkles in shades,
As the laughter now flows,
A bright knapsack of joy,
Where the fun never slows.

Luminous Path to the Soul

A path full of giggles,
With each twinkling light,
Guiding me through fun,
On this wobbly flight.

The stones seem to chuckle,
Under my happy feet,
Every step I take's,
A dance, oh so sweet.

The lanterns all wink,
As they guide me along,
With every step taken,
I find where I belong.

Laughter echoes around,
With each turn I take,
This winding, bright trail,
Is a piece of my cake.

Beacon of Serenity

In a world of chaotic dance,
A compass with a goofy prance.
It points to joy, not fear or fright,
With clumsy grace, it leads to light.

With a twirl and a silly grin,
It tells you where to start, begin.
A wobbly beam that shines so bright,
Twirling stars in the darkest night.

It offers snacks and giggles too,
A buffet of dreams, just for you.
With every laugh, comes a new goal,
A guiding giggle for the soul.

So follow the laugh, it won't mislead,
Where silly flows, you're sure to succeed.
Finding joy in every little scene,
With smiles that dance, and jokes in between.

Whispering Shadows

The shadows dance in silly ways,
They whisper tales of wobbly praise.
Each murmur brings a chuckling sound,
As they prance and play around.

With every flicker, they trip and fall,
Spilling secrets, laughter for all.
A cheeky breeze that teases the night,
Makes every corner a joyful sight.

They tug your sleeve, "Come join the fun!"
In shadowy antics, laughter's begun.
A parade of bumps, slips, and jest,
With shadows laughing, you are blessed.

So heed the whispers, follow the play,
In the midst of the night, let humor sway.
For in each giggle, there's wisdom bright,
That turns every shadow into pure light.

Glowing Echoes of Truth

In the hall of echoes, laughter rings,
Truth wears a crown of funny things.
With echoes bouncing, bouncy and bold,
Each secret seen turns to laughter gold.

Tales twist and twirl, in comical glee,
Showing honesty wrapped in jubilee.
With every giggle, the truth unfolds,
In a chorus of chuckles, the heart beholds.

A jester's wink, a knowing gaze,
Guiding through life's quirky maze.
Beneath the humor, wisdom shines,
In the maze of giggles, joy entwines.

So dance with echoes, don't hesitate,
Truth can be funny, don't wait, don't wait!
In laughter's embrace, we find our way,
Through glowing truths that save the day.

The Radiant Pursuit

On a chase for light, oh what a ride,
In a whirligig world, we slide and glide.
With radiant giggles lighting the trail,
Every twist and turn, we merrily sail.

With a skip, a hop, and a silly grin,
In the foolishness, the joy begins.
Each glowing step is a playful feat,
Where laughter's rhythm and fun will meet.

Through the scrumptious wonders of goofy sights,
We wander beneath the twinkling lights.
In the radiant chase, we find our cheer,
With giggles echoing, the way is clear.

So join the pursuit, take a leap today,
For in giggles found, we learn to sway.
Chasing the fun, let worries dissolve,
In the laughter's light, we truly evolve.

Glowing Heartbeat

In the dark, I peek and seek,
A flicker here, a shadow meek.
With giggles soft and glowing bright,
I chase the charm through silly night.

My friend just tripped, a perfect fall,
Light on his nose—oh, how we squall!
A dance of sparks, a playful show,
We stumble 'round with hearts aglow.

The night folks laugh, they wiggle too,
Their lanterns bob like a wild zoo.
With every step, a joyful prance,
In this twinkling, quirky dance.

So here we skip, no need for plan,
Just glowing hearts, and fun we span.
With every light, a silly cheer,
We frolic on, with none to fear.

Twilight's Guiding Whisper

In twilight's spark, we make a fuss,
Our shadows blend, and yet discuss.
A tiny bat who thinks he's big,
Mistakes our hat for a flying pig!

We snicker when the glow bugs play,
And dance around without delay.
With every whisper, funny tales,
As crazy whims fill night's fine trails.

My hat is lost, it flies away,
In search of fun, it went astray.
Chasing laughs in muffled sound,
The twilight secrets we have found.

Oh, silly moments, lost and found,
In little laughs, our joy is crowned.
In whispers soft and giggles light,
Together we shall greet the night.

Lantern of Quietude

Oh quiet time, you sneak in sly,
With lantern glow, I cannot lie.
It plays a tune with gentle cheer,
But sends my cat into a queer!

A pounce, a bounce, she swats the light,
While I just sit, it's quite the sight.
Her mission's clear, she rules the room,
In shadows thick, she plots her doom.

With every flicker, there's a flash,
As she goes hunting, quick and brash.
Her tiny paws all out of sync,
A funny chase, our spirits link.

So here we laugh in our cocoon,
With lantern glow beneath the moon.
In quiet moments, laughter blooms,
And silliness resumes the rooms.

Flame Beneath the Surface

A sparkle hides beneath the skin,
With every jest, we start to spin.
The glow below, it prompts a smile,
In goofy jokes, we linger awhile.

Oh, bobbing flames, they wink and sway,
Drawing out laughter in bright display.
A little dance upon the floor,
With every step, we lighten more.

With whispers warm and chuckles pure,
Our funny tales, they reassured.
As flames of folly glide and race,
We find our joy in silly space.

Together we'll laugh till morning light,
With twinkling eyes, our spirits bright.
In every flicker, glee reveals,
The flame beneath, our heart it steals.

The Quest for Radiance

In a forest of giggles and gleeful chats,
I searched for a glow, my fancy was spats.
With a map made of jellies and candy so sweet,
I stumbled on laughter, my quest was complete!

Through the trees, old wise owls gave a hoot,
'Follow the breadcrumbs, you silly old brute!'
I danced with the shadows, cheered by the sun,
Who knew finding glimmers could be so much fun?

I chased after fireflies, catching them all,
With a net made of pizza and hair from a doll.
The glow turned to giggles, oh what a sight,
In my quest for the radiance, I found pure delight!

With my lantern of laughter, I lit up the night,
And the creatures all smiled with sheer delight.
For the brightest of lanterns, you see, my dear friend,
Are the smiles we wear and the joys that won't end!

Light of Inner Journeys

I took a wrong turn on the road to my heart,
With a guide made of marshmallows, sweet as a tart.
Each step was a hiccup, I laughed as I tripped,
Who knew my soul journey was all chocolate-dipped?

In the mirror, my dreams had a playful tweak,
They stuck out their tongues and started to speak.
With a giggle, they showed me the dance of my fate,
I spun 'round and 'round, in an inner debate.

A compass of chuckles led me through the maze,
Where pixies threw parties in magical ways.
Every path had a punchline, every turn was a smile,
On this journey of nonsense, I stayed for a while!

So here's to the glow of ridiculous glee,
That shines brightest within, don't you see?
When we follow our laughter, our joy starts to swell,
In this light of our journey, all goes very well!

Guiding Light in Twilight

As the sun slipped away with a wink and a sigh,
I made a pet rock my best friend nearby.
We wandered through twilight, sharing our dreams,
And stumbled on fireflies with cream-filled beams.

The shadows threw parties, they invited the stars,
We jived with the night in our comical cars.
Each blink of a star was a laugh in disguise,
Throwing glittery puns down from the skies.

A lantern of laughter hung high in the trees,
Playing hide and seek with the giggling breeze.
Step on a branch, and it squeaked like a shoe,
I could not help laughing; oh, what can I do?

So we danced through the darkness, our spirits aglow,
With the funny bright lanterns all over the show.
In the twilight of chuckles, we found our bright flame,
For the glow of the night plays a wonderful game!

Echoes of Hopeful Tides

In the breezy cocoon of a whimsical cove,
The waves told me secrets, the sea was my stove.
They bubbled like soda, tickling my toes,
With each splash of joy, the laughter still grows.

A lighthouse of chuckles stood tall on the shore,
With jokes of the ocean, I couldn't ignore.
It flickered like laughter, sent ripples my way,
And each wave that crashed had a funny bouquet.

I surfed on my dreams like a clown on a board,
With a grin made of gumdrops, I never got bored.
The tides sang in puns, a melody bright,
My compass was laughter, guiding me right!

As I rode on the echoes of hopeful delight,
I saw that the lanterns are really our light.
For the joy that we carry, like waves on the sea,
Is the spark of our lives, wild and free!

Flicker of Understanding

In a world so dim and twisted,
Laughter sparks when least expected.
With flickers bright, we start to see,
The humor in our oddity.

Through shadows deep, we dance and play,
Stumbling often on our way.
We giggle at the bumps we find,
And lighten up the muddled mind.

Each misstep turns to joy, it seems,
As we unravel our wild dreams.
Bright ideas come from playful minds,
In the chaos, clarity binds.

So let your heart with humor lift,
In every fumble, find a gift.
For laughter shines in darkest nights,
And guides us with its happy lights.

Glint of Possibility

A glint appears in places strange,
Suggesting life needs a good change.
A wink from fate, a quirky jibe,
Invites us all to join the vibe.

With giggles ringing, plans unfold,
And silly dreams begin to mold.
A spark ignites in crazy ways,
We stumble through the funniest days.

In every twist, a chance is found,
With laughter echoing all around.
So grab your dreams, don't be afraid,
For joy's the light that won't get fade.

Let's chase those glints with playful hearts,
And join together in life's arts.
For humor shines both wild and free,
Opening doors, just wait and see!

The Light Within

Deep within, a beacon glows,
A quirky flame that always knows.
In silly thoughts and playful schemes,
It spins our wildest, wackiest dreams.

With every chuckle, visions dance,
A light that helps us take a chance.
It whispers, 'Don't take life too serious,'
And teaches us to be delirious.

So let it shine, the light we hold,
Through giggles shared and tales retold.
For in the chaos of our play,
The inner glow shows us the way.

In laughter's warmth, we blaze our trails,
Creating joy in silly tales.
So trust the shine, embrace the fun,
And let your light illuminate everyone!

Radiant Path of Reflections

Bright reflections dance upon the ground,
Where laughter echoes, joy is found.
A twist, a turn, a giggle shared,
The path ahead is brightly flared.

With every step, absurdity leads,
As we plant our comical seeds.
And through the puddles, splashes squeal,
Life's a joke, the punchline's real!

In this radiant, silly spree,
We see the world with hilarity.
The winks of fate, the nods of jest,
Create a path that feels the best.

As mirrors show our goofy grins,
We skip along, forgetting sins.
With laughter lighting every turn,
We find the joy for which we yearn.

Light in the Labyrinth

In a maze of socks and shoes,
You'll find some clues and lose some blues.
With every twist, a laugh we share,
Pointing the way like an old bear.

A compass spins, it can't decide,
Which way to go, what path to ride.
We bump our heads on walls of cheer,
And giggles echo loud and clear.

There's always snacks in every nook,
Like little treasures in a book.
With silly paths that make us grin,
We'll dance right out when we're let in.

In the end, we'll break the rules,
And celebrate our wandering fools.
With laughter bright, we'll shine the way,
Through endless fun, come what may.

Ageless Glimmer

In a jar of jellybeans so bright,
We find our wisdom, pure delight.
The flavors mix, a tasty guide,
To giggles shared, and hearts open wide.

Each memory shines like a candy hue,
With laughter's glow, we'll never be blue.
Crackers crunched in an endless cheer,
As we toast the years that brought us here.

With age brings jokes that seem so new,
Like dad jokes told by old Aunt Sue.
We sip sweet tea in the afternoon,
As time slips by like a merry tune.

Our calico cat chases her tail,
While we laugh until we turn pale.
With every wink, the stories play,
In ageless joy, we lose our way.

Campfire of the Soul

Around the fire, we roast marshmallows,
While telling tales that make us bellow.
The smoke spirals up, a silly dance,
As we burst into laughter, what a chance!

With songs that echo under the stars,
We forget our worries, count our jars.
A squirrel joins in, quite confused,
He steals our snacks, a snack thief excused!

We swap those ghost tales, full of wit,
And wonder if it's time to commit.
To roasting more bites or swapping flair,
With love and laughter warming the air.

The night grows old, our voices soar,
In our little world, we ask for more.
With every laugh, we light the way,
In this endless night, we choose to play.

Radiance of Forgotten Dreams

In dusty corners, dreams lie still,
We poke at them with sheer goodwill.
They flutter up like butterflies,
With silly smiles and sparkly eyes.

Each wish we made, a playful tease,
Like jumping jacks and summer breeze.
We dance around and sing out loud,
As former dreams join in the crowd.

Forgotten balloon animals bounce,
With cheerful squeaks, they leap and pounce.
We polish them with giggles bright,
And watch them spin in pure delight.

The floppy hats and mismatched shoes,
Remind us laughter's the best news.
With radiant joy, we take a leap,
In dreams revived, our hearts will keep.

The Wisdom Flame

A flickering light in the night,
Dodging all shadows, what a sight!
It whispers of stories, old and new,
Reminding us to cherish our crew.

When you stumble and trip on your shoes,
Just follow the glow, you can't lose!
It teases and dances, showing the way,
While cracking jokes about yesterday's fray.

Like a wise old owl with a cheeky grin,
It nudges your heart to let laughter in.
If life brings you troubles, don't take it too hard,
Just remember this flame won't leave you jarred.

So grasp its warmth, let it beckon your cheer,
For wisdom ignites when we're lighthearted, my dear!

Celestial Glow at Dusk

Stars in the sky play hide and seek,
With giggles and twinkles, oh-so-unique!
The moon takes a bow, feeling quite grand,
As laughter floats gently across the land.

Glowbugs are fashionably late to the show,
Wearing their sparkles; a heavenly glow!
They waltz through the air like party balloons,
While we dance in circles, howling at moons.

The twilight's a canvas, painted with dreams,
As silly thoughts bubble like frothy cream.
So toss your worries into the night,
And let your heart take wing—what a flight!

With a chuckle or two, under starlit embrace,
We'll toast to the glow, and the joy in our space!

Radiant Echoes of the Past

In the attic I found an old bottle of light,
It whispered to me, 'Don't give up the fight!'
With echoes of laughter from days long ago,
It tickled my heart like a friendly show.

A relic of wisdom, with winks and a sway,
It guided my dreams like a dance at ballet.
Poking fun at my fumbles, it shimmered with glee,
Sparking the mischief that lives deep in me.

It jests about choices that birthed funny tales,
Navigating life with whimsical trails.
So toast to the past, with a wink and a grin,
For every bright blunder brings joy from within!

Glow on, dear memories, don't ever depart,
Your radiant echoes will always warm the heart!

A Glow in the Fog

Amidst the thick fog that blankets the street,
A glimmering light shows the way with a beat.
It twirls in the haze, a shy little star,
Leading the lost, never too far.

With chuckles and giggles, it flits to and fro,
While I trip over puddles—oh, such a show!
Every step forward is a dance and a jest,
This glow holds a secret—my chaotic quest!

It nudges me gently, whispers, "Don't stew,
There's laughter in stumble; it's good for you!"
So I twirl through the mist, my heart light and free,
Winking at shadows, just my glow and me.

In the fog, we unite with chuckles galore,
A glowing companion—who could ask for more?

Guiding Flames of Intuition

In shadows deep, we often roam,
With sparks of thought, we find our home.
If you trip on a shoe, just laugh it off,
Your mind's bright glow will show where to scoff!

An itch, a twitch, what could it mean?
Maybe it's tacos, not your routine.
Follow your nose, when in a bind,
It's the best GPS you'll ever find!

A chuckle here, a giggle there,
Together we'll travel, without a care.
With heart and laughter, we navigate
Through silly mistakes, our dreams await!

So let's embrace the joy we see,
With whims of fancy and quirky glee.
We'll dance with sparks that brightly flare,
Intuition's flame—let's breathe the air!

The Celestial Navigator

Up above, the stars do wink,
While I'm underfoot, losing my drink!
A cosmic guide? I thought it was free,
Instead, it's just some ants chasing me!

Sailing on dreams, I catch a breeze,
But then trip over my own two knees.
With planets swirling in a jolly spin,
I navigate through where I've been!

Comets whiz by, while I hum a tune,
Who knew the path was lit by the moon?
Galaxies giggle, they can't look away,
From my majestic dance on the Milky Way!

When the cosmos chuckle, I just can't lie,
They know the stars keep us flying high.
With a wink and a nudge, I'll find my mark,
Thanks to the universe, I'm never in the dark!

Flickering Dreams in the Night

Beneath the covers, I plot my scheme,
Chasing those dreams, or so it would seem.
But wait! What's that, a cat on my head?
Guess which way my dream boat is led!

With sleep in my eyes, the visions dance,
A world so silly, I give it a chance.
Unicorns prance through the streets at noon,
While I run late, singing off-tune!

A flicker of joy as the night rolls on,
Who knew dreams could be this much fun?
I ride on a toaster, it flies quite right,
But then I wake up, where's my kite?

So, off I go to chase that cheer,
Into the wild laughter we hold dear.
With flickering thoughts aglow in the night,
We'll keep on dreaming, and that feels just right!

Lighthouses of the Heart

When storms arise, I chart my course,
With giggles and grins as my strong force.
These beacons shine, so playful and bright,
Guiding my way with pure delight!

An old joke here, a pun there,
With laughter that floats upon the air.
I steer through waves of ticklish fun,
Navigating life; I'm never done!

Open my heart, it's a lighthouse strong,
With all my quirks, I can't go wrong.
From silliness blooms a radiant spark,
Laughter leads me through the dark!

So here we stand, hand in hand,
Facing the tides, our dreams so grand.
Through storms and laughter, fun's our part,
In this great journey, we light the heart!

The Nurturing Flame

In a cozy nook, on a winter's night,
Sits a candle, glowing so bright.
It flickers and dances, like it's got a tease,
Whispers of warmth, putting us at ease.

The shadows play, a quirky ballet,
As we munch on snacks, brightening our day.
It sighs with delight, as if it can chat,
Lighting up laughter, just imagine that!

In that gentle glow, secrets are told,
Of pizza toppings and fortune untold.
With each little flicker, our giggles expand,
Oh, the stories we craft with a warm candle's hand!

So here we gather, under its reign,
In the company of light, none can complain.
A funny little beacon that shows us the way,
To cozy delights and a bright, jolly play!

Spark of Life's Journey

In the realm of dreams, where ideas ignite,
A spark flares up in the dead of the night.
It trips on the carpet, says, 'Oops, my bad!'
And giggles softly, thinking this is rad.

With each little puff, it takes flight anew,
Dodging the chores, oh what a view!
It whispers sweet nothings with a sly little grin,
As socks and lost keys start to swim in.

As we ride this wave of chaotic delight,
Clinging to dreams that lift us so bright.
The spark of our journey, in whimsical tone,
Turns messes to magic, in its silly zone!

So let's laugh together, as we fumble and sway,
With a spark in our hearts, come what may!
In the light of adventure, we waltz together,
Finding joy in the journey, like birds of a feather!

Light that Knows No Bounds

From the depths of the fridge, a glow shines so clear,
It's the leftover pizza, my motivation, dear!
With cheese like the sun and crust like a dream,
It beckons me closer, or so it would seem.

As I stumble at midnight, it leads me with glee,
Guiding my hands like a mystical sea.
A beacon of hope in the kitchen late-night,
Making 3 AM mishaps taste right with each bite!

I giggle aloud, as I savor my prize,
With toppings of joy, oh how they surprise!
With each hearty munch, my worries take flight,
In the glow of old dinner, everything feels right.

So here's to the light that warms and astounds,
In unexpected places, joy knows no bounds.
Like pizza at midnight, or cake left to share,
In the lights of our life, good humor's everywhere!

The Guiding Gaze of Stars

At the edge of the world, where twinkles align,
Stars cast their wishes, a celestial sign.
They giggle and wink, saying, 'Follow the bright!'
As we chase after dreams in the lush, starry night.

With a map made of laughter and stardust in hand,
We navigate life like a whimsical band.
Each star a companion on this silly ride,
Whispers of joy that are bursting with pride.

They light up the dark, like a fun parade,
Showing us pathways where mischief is made.
With constellations pointing, we dance and we spin,
As the cosmos giggles, we feel the delight within.

So let's stay enchanted, under this radiant show,
In the laughter of starlight, our happiness grows.
As we swirl through the night, with whimsy unbound,
The guiding gaze of stars, our laughter is found!

The Lightkeeper's Promise

In the night, I swear to glow,
Yet sometimes I trip on my toe.
With every flicker, a giggle's heard,
As I chase shadows like a silly bird.

My lantern's bright, or so they say,
But it's often wrong, leading astray.
A wink to the moths, all fly in a race,
In my bright beam, they find their place.

When fog rolls in, I give a shout,
"Is anyone there? Come on out!"
But only the echoes reply to my call,
And a wayward cat thinks it's a ball.

I promise to guide with a comical spin,
And bring out a laugh with the light from within.
For what use is glow with too much fright?
Let's chuckle together till the morning light!

Beacons of the Unseen

Here's to lights that wink and blink,
Under the stars, we laugh, we think.
Those beams that dance in strange designs,
Make even the shadows wear funny lines.

A quirky glow from a lamp posts a joke,
As I trip on a root while I giggle and poke.
'Who needs a map?' the lantern sings,
'Just follow me—unless trouble springs!'

Eyes all squinted in the night's glow,
With every step, I'm sure to stow
A blast of laughter as I mislead,
Into a bush, where giggles breed.

So raise a toast to guides unseen,
Who shimmy like stars in a silly routine.
For every twist and turn we find,
We craft a tale, both bright and blind!

Shadows Danced by Light

In the moonlit glow, shadows prance,
A wiggly dance, a funny chance.
They tiptoe around with gleeful delight,
Competing with beams in a humorous fight.

My lantern's bright, yet sway it can't,
So I laugh as I guide with a silly chant.
'This way, my friends, don't you fall!
Unless the bushes get the last call.'

In jest, the darkness plays peek-a-boo,
While flickering lights cast silly views.
A laugh here and there, with shadows in tow,
Lighthearted moments in a whimsical show.

So round we go, we clumsily sway,
With each wooden step, we lighten the way.
Bringing charm to the night, while humor's alive,
In a flicker of fun, we flourish and thrive!

Navigators of the Inner Voyage

On a boat made of giggles, we sail the night,
Guided by glimmers, such a silly sight.
With lanterns aglow, we map out the stars,
But end up drifting to places like Mars.

Each wave a chuckle that shakes up the crew,
As the captain yells, "To the jellyfish, loo!"
With lanterns that sway and leap in delight,
We crash through the dreams of the comical night.

The compass spins wildly, it grins at our strife,
As we navigate dreams in the fun of our life.
'Just follow the light!' I tell my dear mates,
Into the horizon, where laughter awaits.

So onward we journey, no need for a fight,
With a giggle to spare in the magical night.
Guided by beams that tickle the soul,
We shimmer and shine, on a roll!

The Gentle Glow of Remembrance

In a cozy nook, I sit and ponder,
About the times that take me yonder.
A light that flickers, makes me chuckle,
Recalling moments, like a playful buckle.

A silly hat, a dance so grand,
Gleeful faces, hand in hand.
Each gentle flicker brings a smile,
Reminding me to stay awhile.

Oh, the laughter shared with glee,
The pranks we pulled, just you and me.
A glow shines bright within my core,
As memories dance and laughter soars.

So here's to the glow, sweet and mild,
Recalling antics, like a child.
With every whimsy, every jest,
The warm remembrance, I love the best.

Pilgrimage of the Radiant Flame

On a journey bright, I stroll with flare,
A candle's glow, I stop and stare.
Wobbling lightly as I traverse,
I think, perhaps, this is the verse!

With giggles here and snorts out there,
This radiant flame, it has no care.
Beneath its light, I trip and fall,
And chuckle loudly, no pride at all.

I wander through this quirky path,
Whispers of humor, no aftermath.
Each flicker laughs, and winks in jest,
This glow, indeed, is the very best.

In this pilgrimage, what fun we find,
Illuminated laughter, sweet and kind.
Oh, the radiant flame, we dance along,
With joy in our hearts, oh how we belong!

Guiding Hands in the Twilight

In twilight's hue, with playful cheer,
Guiding hands, oh my dear!
With a wink and a giggle, we march ahead,
No need for maps, just laughter instead!

Through bumps and giggles, we take our flight,
Navigating joy in soft twilight.
Each glow is like a guiding friend,
In hilarious moments, our troubles end.

We trip and tumble, what a sight,
Those guiding hands keeping spirits light.
With silly hats and antics galore,
In this world of twilight, we simply adore!

So here's to friendship, laughter's embrace,
Guiding us both at a playful pace.
With every turn, let laughter reign,
In the twilight's charm, we dance again!

Lanterns of Resilience

In the darkest nights, we shine so bright,
Lanterns swaying, oh what a sight!
With laughter piled in layers thick,
We bounce back quick, oh what a trick!

From fumbles and flops, we rise with glee,
These lanterns of joy, they're wild and free.
With each little flame, a giggle ignites,
Battling shadows, oh what delights!

As we dance through storms, we spin and sway,
With lanterns held high, come what may!
Through thick and thin, we find our way,
Resilient spirits brightening the fray.

Here's to laughter, come blunders and falls,
We'll light up the night with our silly calls.
In resilience's glow, we forge ahead,
With giggles and grins, our worries shed!

Celestial Guidance

In the dark, a glow appears,
Like a moth that sips its beers.
It wobbles left, it sways on right,
A star that's lost but still in sight.

It laughs and hiccups, makes me grin,
Telling tales of where it's been.
"Wander this way, don't trip on shoes!"
While I question, "Do I really choose?"

Watch out for clouds, they block the view,
Like that time I lost my shoe!
A dance of fate, a silly cheer,
Guided by light, I have no fear.

With every twist, a giggling sound,
In this haze, my joy is found.
Chasing beams that shift and play,
I'll find my path, come what may!

Radiance Amidst Shadows

In the gloom, it shines so bright,
A wandering spark on a crazy flight.
"Follow me, I've got a plan!"
But I just tripped on that tarpan.

It zigzags past, with such delight,
Saying, "Keep up, this is alright!"
But all I see are dancing trees,
I just hope they don't have fleas!

A shimmer here, a wavy twist,
With every glow, a silly mist.
In shadows deep, we chase our fate,
While giggling at a bashful crate.

So let us dance through darkened nights,
With rumbling bellies and odd delights.
Radiance bright, let's find our ways,
Laughing through these twilight days!

Flickering Essence

A flicker here, a flicker there,
Like a candle with wild hair.
It sparks and flies, it takes a chance,
Inviting all for a quirky dance.

"Just follow me, don't lose your hat!"
It chirps along with a funny chat.
Twists and turns, it might just fall,
But laughs instead — oh what a ball!

In a world that's full of tricks,
It's leading me with jiggly flicks.
"Over here, don't trip on that!"
As I hop over a sleeping cat.

With every bob, I find some cheer,
This guiding light is far from drear.
Let's wander off, with giggles near,
And let this flicker steer us clear!

The Compass of the Heart

A compass spins, oh what a tease,
Pointing north towards the cheese.
"To the left!" it squeaks with glee,
While I just wish to sit and flee.

With every whirl, it acts like a clown,
"Dance this way, let's spin around!"
I trip on my laces, tumble down,
This silly compass wears a crown!

So onward we go, at this weird pace,
Through laughter lines, our silly race.
"Don't lose heart, but maybe shoes,"
It giggles softly, "you can't choose!"

But in the end, as night does fall,
We find our way, goofing through it all.
With a compass bright, we laugh and sing,
In this chaos, joy is the thing!

Light Beneath the Shadows

In corners dark where lost socks roam,
A flicker dances, calling them home.
It giggles and chuckles, saying, "Don't fret!"
With a wink and a nudge, it's our light-hearted pet.

It brightens the path to the fridge at night,
Guiding me gently to marshmallow delight.
I stumble and trip, but it stays right there,
A sarcastic glimmer, not a single care.

When the mood gets low and the ice cream's all gone,
It throws out some jokes, and we linger till dawn.
Through shadows it prances, on feet made of glee,
Laughing together, just my light and me.

So here's to the glow that keeps humor alive,
The flickers of laughter that help us survive.
In the darkest of moments, it sparks a delight,
Brightening shadows with each silly light.

Whispering Beacons of Hope

Glowing through chaos with a sparkle and grin,
It whispers sweet nothings, come on, jump in!
As I fumble and stumble, it giggles in glee,
"Who knew you'd trip on a banana peel, me?"

A glow that ignites with each silly mishap,
Reminding me gently, life needs a good laugh.
With a flicker and fade, it dances with zest,
Who needs a guide when it's here for a jest?

Like fireflies flashing in quirky array,
It plays tag with shadows, making dark jump away.
A lighthouse of chuckles on tempestuous seas,
Each wave brings a wink, bringing laughter with ease.

Oh, the glow that accompanies the clumsy and bold,
In laughter and joy, a new story unfolds.
In a world painted gray, it rings like a chime,
Whispering hope wrapped in giggles and rhyme.

Lanterns of the Lost

Underneath cushions where coins tend to hide,
A lanterns of lost things, swift as a glide.
It's snickering sweetly at my puzzled face,
"Looking for your wallet? Try a different place!"

With beams full of mischief, it plays hide and seek,
"Why don't you check where those odd socks peek?"
In closets and cubbies, it throws back its head,
"Found a tater tot? Here, let's share instead!"

Each lost little doodad comes alive with delight,
As this glowing companion turns mischief to light.
Turn that frown upside down, join in this spree,
What's lost is now found—with laughs, not decree.

So here's to the lantern that misses some cues,
And brings back the treasures beneath daily blues.
Through chaos and clutter, it shines with a grin,
A beacon of joy with each jumbled win!

Illuminating the Soul's Path

It twinkles and sparkles on the road of the wise,
With a wink and a nod, it opens my eyes.
Stepping on gum and puddles with flair,
"Watch your step, buddy! It's a sticky affair!"

With a chuckle, it leads, playing tricks as we go,
"Take that left at the cactus, avoid the crow's show!"
In a twisty old path that's full of surprise,
I follow its glow while it rolls its bright eyes.

Glancing at shadows that stretch far and wide,
"Look at that! A raccoon in a silly ride!"
In moments of worry, it lights up the space,
"Silly ol' fella, don't wear that old face!"

So with giggles and laughter, we soar through the maze,
This glow guides my steps in the funniest ways.
With joy in the journey and smiles that last,
The light in my heart shines bright, unsurpassed.

Shadow's Embrace

In the night, shadows creep,
They giggle and jump, making me leap.
With a wink and a nudge, they call my name,
I laugh as they play their silly game.

A moonlit dance, they prance around,
Tickling my toes, their joy profound.
With every flicker, they steal my breath,
In their playful grip, I flirt with death.

They whisper secrets, oh so sly,
Chasing my worries, they flit by.
With a dash of mischief, they lead the way,
In their silly charm, I'm eager to stay.

Oh, shadows, dear friends, in their sweet way,
They remind me to live, to laugh and to play.
For every twirl in the moonlit hue,
Brings giggles and glee, a joy so true.

The Luminous Wayfinder

A glow in the fog, oh what a sight,
Bouncing and bobbing, it's pure delight.
With a giggle and jiggle, it calls me near,
"Come on, my friend, let's conquer this fear!"

We trot through the dark, like two clumsy clowns,
It leads me through streets without any frowns.
With every bright step, the world seems so fun,
Who knew that this journey could have just begun?

It twirls and it swirls, with each little tease,
Taking me places where laughter's a breeze.
Finding the joy in the littlest things,
Under moonlight's gaze, where the happiness sings.

So here's to the glow, so playful and bright,
A wayfinder's laughter, my heart takes flight.
In the dance of the dark, I'm led to the light,
With joy ever present, all wrongs feel so right.

Luminary of Resilience

In a world so dark, with socks unmatched,
I found a flashlight, my quest soon hatched.
Through puddles and giggles, I marched on bright,
Illuminating woes with my new found light.

My cat looked confused, at this glowing beam,
Chasing shadows like they're part of a dream.
I twirled and I laughed, dancing like a fool,
For resilience shines, even as a tool.

Each stumble was met with a comical bounce,
As I flicked the switch, darkness tried to pounce.
With every bright flicker, I'd trip and I'd laugh,
In the game of my life, I'm the brightest giraffe.

So here's to the laughter that follows each glow,
In the oddest of moments, we learn to grow.
With resilience, we smile, and though we may fall,
Our luminary hearts can inspire us all.

Illumination in the Abyss

In the depths of the night, where the shadows play,
I tripped on a root that led me astray.
A flicker appeared, with a wink and a smile,
Saying, "Keep moving, kid, just go that extra mile!"

With a basket of fries and a dream on my plate,
The darkness could not dim my appetite's fate.
As I munched and I laughed, watching shadows dance,
I knew in my heart, I'd give life a chance.

A quirky old ghost, with a plan so absurd,
Joined me on my quest, not a single word heard.
Together we twinkled, like stars in the gloom,
Taking over the night, with our glow and our boom.

So let's light up the dark, with our giggles and cheer,
For even in abyss, there's a case for good beer!
In the depth of the night, the fun won't decline,
With oddball companions, we'll savor the shine.

Guiding Light Through Time

Tick tock, it's time for a whimsical ride,
Through moments of madness, with laughter as pride.
In my time machine, I've got popcorn galore,
With a button for laughter—let's open the door!

I bumped into Newton, he dropped his own pie,
And laughed at my blinking, "What's wrong with the
sky?"
With time all around us, we danced like mad kids,
Building castles from clouds, with our imaginations' bids.

We boogied with cavemen, those funky rock stars,
With lights in our pockets, we traveled to Mars.
In the glow of the future, we're never in strife,
For the giggles we cherish all brighten our life.

As we zip through the ages, with joy as our guide,
Laughter's the secret, the spark we won't hide.
In every tick-tock, let the humor unfold,
For life is our lantern, more precious than gold.

Flickering Lamplight

In a cozy old room, with a flicker of flame,
I found my lost sock, oh what a shame!
It danced on the table, in a waltz all its own,
"Look at me now!" it said, "I'm never alone!"

With biscuits and stories, and tea in my cup,
The light played magician, lifting me up.
Each shadow a joker, performing a jest,
As I chuckled along, finding peace in my nest.

With every small flicker, the laughter grew bold,
In a world so unsure, my joy never cold.
Candles and giggles, a party of sorts,
Where darkness can't linger, just fun retorts.

So let's laugh at the flicker, embrace the slight shake,
In the glow of the magic, we're wide awake.
For in every dim corner, there's a joke to ignite,
With flickering lamplight, our spirits take flight.

Guiding Flicker Through Fear

In the dark, I hear a squeak,
My socks are wet, my knees are weak.
A light flickers, yellow strain,
Is it a bug or just my brain?

I tiptoe through the shadowed hall,
Where laughter echoes, spirits call.
A glow emerges, with a wink,
It's just my cat, I need a drink!

At midnight snacks, I find delight,
With cookie crumbs, I start a fight.
But wait, what's that? A shadow creeps,
It's just the fridge that loudly beeps!

My guiding flicker, ever near,
Turns all my doubt into good cheer.
So if you fear a ghostly banter,
Just blame it on the cat—a dancer!

Elysium's Luminescence

A glow that spills across the floor,
Is it a trick or something more?
A zap of light from my old lamp,
Or dreams of cheese—oh, that sweet stamp!

In a world where shadows prance,
A disco ball gives me a chance.
With every twirl, I make my way,
And dodge the cat that wants to play!

The fridge hums loud, a melody,
A symphony of yogurt glee.
I twirl around with snacks in hand,
A waltz of joy, oh wasn't planned!

So here I dance, not a care to measure,
With every flicker, I find my pleasure.
In radiant glow, I laugh and cheer,
Elysium shines when friends are near!

Dawn's Tender Glow

The sun peeks in, what a sight,
I'm still wrapped up, oh what a fight!
Pajamas stuck, hair in a mess,
But hey, who cares? I won't stress!

Bright rays dance across my floor,
A woodpecker's knock—what's there in store?
Coffee brews with a cheerful pop,
A little jig, I can't just stop!

I spill my drink, a tiny splash,
The dog leaps up, it's quite the crash!
Together laughing, we share the cheer,
Dawn's tender glow brings friends near.

With giggles bright, we start anew,
Morning antics, just me and you.
In every ray, we find our play,
Oh what a bright, hilarious day!

Eternal Light of Purpose

Out in the garden, I take my stroll,
A lightning bug plays, what a silly goal!
It flicks and flitters, right out of line,
Is it a bug, or was that just mine?

With purpose bright, I plant a seed,
But lost my plans, oh dear, oh me!
A squirrel leaps, with acorn in tow,
A grand buffet, come on, let's go!

I chase that critter, round and round,
Tumbling over and onto the ground.
In my quest for light and fun,
I trip and laugh, it's never done!

With each misstep, a chuckle grows,
Eternal joy in silly woes.
In every stumble, I find my way,
A guiding light in games we play!

Illuminated Pathways

In a world so dark and dreary,
I stumbled upon something cheery.
A little light, oh what a sight,
Led me to pizza, wow, what a night!

I followed it down wobbly lanes,
Avoiding the puddles, and the trains.
It giggled and danced, then served me cake,
This kooky light, what a funny break!

It pulled me to friends with silly hats,
Who played on a stage, juggling cats.
Each laugh a spark, each smile a glow,
Who knew guiding lights could put on a show!

So here's to the beams that light our way,
With giggles and grins they lead us astray.
In this wacky world, we shine and prance,
Chasing our dreams, in a luminous dance!

Glimmer in the Darkness

In the depths, where shadows collide,
A flicker appears, and I take it in stride.
With a wink and a grin, it says, "Don't you fret!"
I swear I just saw my cat with a hat!

It bounces around, a spark so spry,
Leading me forth, oh me, oh my!
I stumble and trip, but it laughs with glee,
"Keep up, dear human, come dance with me!"

With each little glow, my fears take flight,
As I chase the glow in the deep of night.
A whimsical guide, oh so light-hearted,
In the play of the dark, I'm joyfully started.

Together we frolic, through chaos and cheer,
I follow that glimmer, no doubt, I have no fear.
For every misstep is a laugh, a tease,
In the light-hearted dark, my worries ease.

Radiant Soul's Compass

Through the mazes of life, my compass spins,
Pointing left, then south, then again it grins.
With its bright little smile, it gives a wink,
"Don't take it too serious, just stop and think!"

It chirps like a bird, leading me wide,
With each silly twist, I take it in stride.
A laugh on the breeze, it dances away,
"Come join the fun! You can't let it sway!"

With a hop and a skip and a dash of flair,
I follow its giggle through the cool night air.
As I trip on my shoelace, it squeaks with delight,
"You're doing just grand! Now, hold on tight!"

Oh joy of direction, so playful and spry,
A compass of laughter that teaches to fly.
With its radiant charm, I'm guided anew,
Through the silly twists, where laughs will ensue.

Whispered Light of Hope

A flickering candle upon the table,
Whispers of joy, if we're willing and able.
It says, 'Don't fret, just take a peek,
There's cake in the fridge! At least a week!'

When shadows loom and gloom begins,
I turn to my buddy, who always grins.
With sparkles of laughter, we chase away doubt,
As the moon beams down, we dance all about!

Lost in the giggles, our worries grow small,
The glimmering light makes us forget it all.
'Twilight or bust!' I yell with glee,
And we trip over nothing—what a sight to see!

This beacon of chuckles brings joy and cheer,
A dazzling reminder that laughter is near.
With whispered wishes and a dash of fun,
We'll laugh till the end, our journey's begun!

Flame of the Unfathomed

On a hill where oddities frolic and play,
I found a flame that led me astray.
With a cap and a bow, it danced on the grass,
Asking, 'Why not join? Don't let life pass!'

It twirled in circles, it blinked with style,
A flamboyant fireball, come chat for a while.
It rattled off jokes, oh what a delight,
'The punchline is yours, just hold on tight!'

So off we pranced, through the bubbles of night,
Tickling the stars, feeling oh-so-right.
This unpredictable flame, so quirky and wild,
Led me to dreams that made me feel like a child!

With every new giggle, the darkness did wane,
Beneath a snickering moon, let's dance in the rain.
For life's a big stage, where oddities bloom,
With a flame full of laughter, dispelling all gloom!

Celestial Torch

A torch so bright, it twinkled and blinked,
I thought to myself, 'How did I think?'
In the depths of night, it called for a hike,
With snacks in my pockets, oh, this could be like!

It bobbed through the shadows, a whimsical sprite,
Leading me onward, oh what a sight!
I chuckled aloud, as we scaled the steep,
Every step more clumsy, diving into the deep!

Who knew a flame could throw such a party?
It hummed silly tunes, so light and hearty.
Mocking the crickets, all awkward and lame,
It turned wandering paths into a fun game!

So if you should meet this torch so absurd,
Grab a bike or a bubble, it's truly preferred.
For in the night's chaos, the joy is all yours,
With laughter and light, let's open wide doors!

www.ingramcontent.com/pod-product-compliance
Ingram Content Group UK Ltd.
Pitfield, Milton Keynes, MK11 3LW, UK
UKHW022105050225
454743UK00006B/79